Earth's Changing Surface

by Kelly Kong

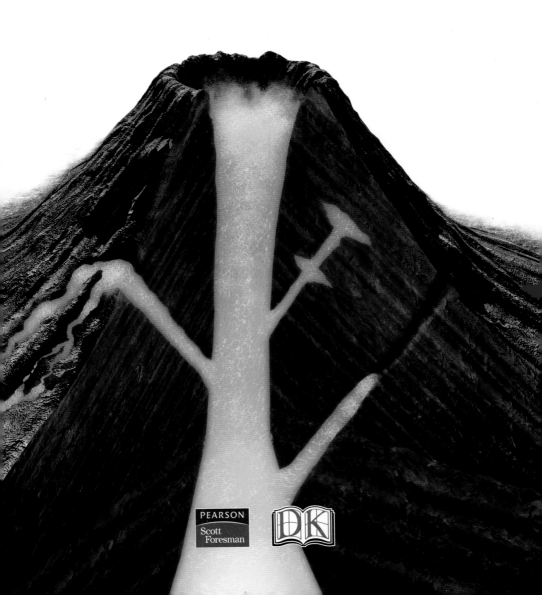

PEARSON
Scott
Foresman

DK

What is the structure of Earth?

The Crust

Earth is made up of four different layers. The **crust** is Earth's thin outer layer. There are two types of crust. Continental crust is found on land and is mostly granite. It is thickest in the mountains, where it can reach a depth of 75 kilometers.

Continental shelf

Continental slope

The crust beneath the ocean floor is called oceanic crust. It is mostly made of a dark green or black rock called basalt. This crust is about 6 to 11 kilometers thick.

Part of the continental crust is underwater. This is called the continental shelf. At the edge of the shelf is a steep drop-off, called the continental slope. At the bottom of this slope is the continental rise, which is the start of the oceanic crust. This is less than 100 kilometers from the coast in most places.

Continental rise

The Mantle and Core

Below the crust is a thick layer called the **mantle.** It makes up most of Earth's material. The top part of the mantle is solid hot rock. This part plus the crust above it form the lithosphere.

Deep in the mantle the pressure is very high. Temperatures range from 360°C to 2,500°C. Rock in this area is solid, but the heat and pressure make it flow like a thick liquid. The hotter rock floats upward as cooler rock sinks. This is a convection current. The lithosphere floats on top of these currents.

The center of Earth is the **core,** which is made mostly of iron. Temperatures in the core can reach 7,000°C. The inner core is solid. The outer core is liquid that flows in currents. These currents make Earth's magnetic field.

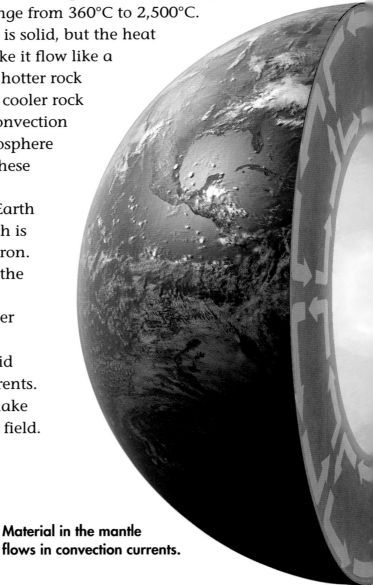

Material in the mantle flows in convection currents.

The mantle and the core are so far below Earth's surface that scientists cannot get there to study them. They learn about these layers in different ways. Scientists study rock from the mantle that comes up through cracks in the crust.

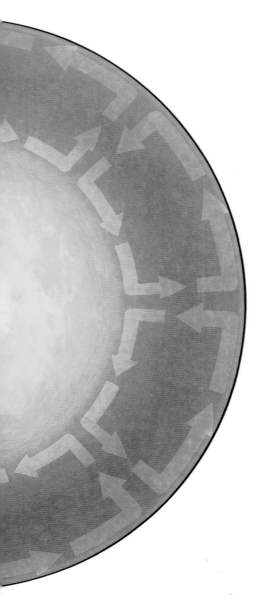

Scientists also learn about Earth's layers by measuring earthquake vibrations with a tool called a seismograph. As vibrations move through the different layers, they change speed and direction. Some stop completely when they reach the outer core. By studying the vibrations from earthquakes everywhere, scientists can learn about Earth's layers.

Scientists can also learn about the mantle and core through laboratory experiments. Materials that are likely inside Earth are tested under great heat and pressure.

What causes earthquakes and volcanoes?

Earth's Plates

The lithosphere is broken up into large and small sections called **plates.** Although you can't feel it, these plates are always moving. A plate may include continents, parts of the ocean floor, or both. Edges of plates are called plate boundaries.

Earth's plates move as slowly as 1 centimeter per year and as fast as 24 centimeters per year. Plates can move into, pull apart from, or grind past each other. These movements change Earth's surface. Mountains and valleys can form. Earthquakes and volcanoes usually happen at plate boundaries.

Plates move for different reasons. Sometimes gravity pulls part of a plate down into the mantle. This pulls the rest of the plate with it. Plates also move due to convection currents in the mantle.

Spreading plate boundary

There are three main types of plate boundaries. Converging plate boundaries are formed where two plates collide. This can build mountains by folding, tilting, or lifting the crust.

Spreading plate boundaries form when plates separate. There is a spreading plate boundary in the middle of the Atlantic Ocean. This ocean is getting wider as the plates move apart. A ridge has formed at the edges of the plates. It has a low area running down its middle, which is called a rift valley.

When two plates slide past each other in opposite directions it is called a sliding plate boundary. Part of California sits on a sliding plate boundary.

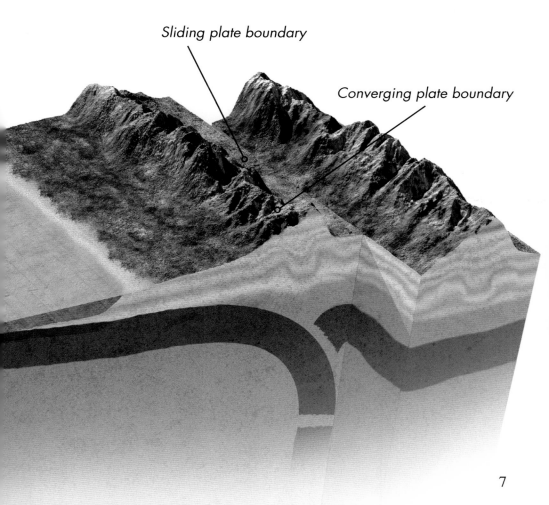

Sliding plate boundary

Converging plate boundary

Earthquakes

Earth's surface is changed by different kinds of forces. Constructive forces build new features like mountains. Destructive forces tear down features. Earthquakes are destructive forces.

Earthquakes usually happen at faults. These are cracks in Earth's crust. As two plates slide past each other, they sometimes get stuck. Pressure builds up, and in time the plates break free. They move suddenly, creating the vibrations of an earthquake. The place where the plates slip is called a focus. The point on Earth's surface above a focus is an epicenter.

Energy released in earthquakes can cause destruction, such as landslides. Most injuries from earthquakes are caused by buildings falling apart. Earthquakes under the ocean can produce huge, dangerous waves called tsunamis.

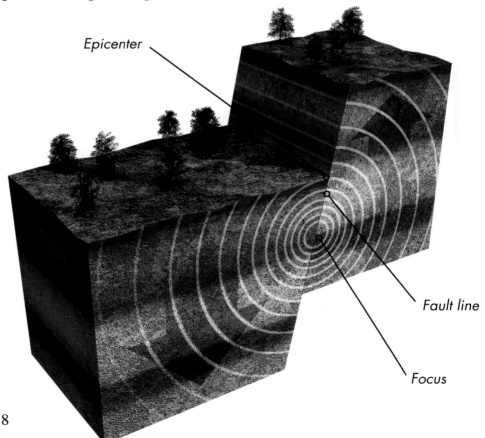

Epicenter

Fault line

Focus

Volcanoes

Most volcanoes form near converging plate boundaries. When one plate slides under another, rock melts into magma. Sometimes magma breaks through weak spots in the crust to reach Earth's surface. The melted rock then flows out as lava. Gases such as water vapor and carbon dioxide can mix with lava. Trapped gases can create pressure and cause a volcano to explode. When this happens, lava can cool in the air and fall as solid rock or ash.

Volcanoes can also form on the ocean floor. If the volcano grows high enough to reach the surface, it becomes an island. This is how the islands of Hawaii were formed. In this case, the volcano is a constructive force.

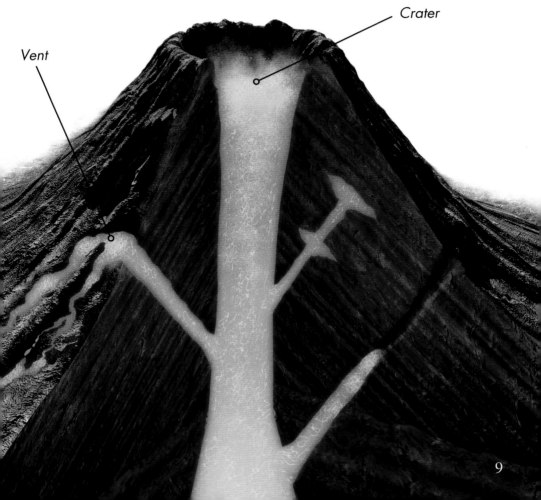

Crater

Vent

What is weathering?

Weathering

Weathering is the process that breaks rocks into smaller pieces called sediments. There are two types of weathering. When gravity, ice, or plant roots break up rocks, it is called **mechanical weathering.** When chemical processes change the rocks, it is called **chemical weathering.**

Mechanical Weathering

Ice wedging occurs when water freezes in cracks in rocks. When wind blows dirt from mountains, the rocks in the mountain are under less pressure. They expand at different rates and cracks form. As cracks grow, water enters them and freezes. The water expands as it freezes, breaking the rocks apart.

This rock has been split by ice wedging.

The rate of mechanical weathering depends on the type of rock and the conditions. Roots can grow into cracks in a rock and push the rock apart. This weathering occurs more quickly in warm, wet conditions, where roots grow faster. The roots will split soft rocks more quickly than hard ones.

Chemical Weathering

Chemicals also break down rocks. Raindrops absorb carbon dioxide from the air. This makes a chemical called carbonic acid. When rain soaks into some rocks, the carbonic acid can dissolve parts of them. Caves can form. Fungi and other organisms can also give off chemicals that change rocks.

Some rocks are more quickly broken down by chemical weathering than others. Areas with lots of rain have more chemical weathering than other areas.

Soil

Soil contains sediment from weathered rocks. It also contains decayed material from organisms, gases from air, and water.

Soil can be red, brown, black, or gray. Soil with larger particles, such as sand, lets water pass through more easily. Soil with smaller particles, such as clay, holds water better and feels smooth. Most plants grow best in soil with a lot of decayed matter.

Topsoil contains a large amount of decayed material.

Subsoil is often a different color than topsoil.

Bedrock is nearly solid rock that lies below the subsoil.

11

What is erosion?

Erosion and Deposition

Erosion is the movement of materials away from a place. Deposition is the placing of materials in a new place. Erosion is a destructive process, while deposition is a constructive one. Sand dunes, valleys, and deltas are formed by erosion and deposition together.

Gravity is the main force that causes erosion. Gravity can cause landslides during earthquakes or after rains. Landslides often occur on steep slopes with no trees. Tree roots help keep soil in place.

Gravity also causes rivers to flow. As river water flows downhill, it picks up sediments. These sediments can wear away the riverbed. Fast-moving rivers can carry heavier sediments and erode deep canyons.

This canyon was formed by erosion.

Erosion from water happens in other places as well. In the ocean, currents can erode deep valleys in the continental shelf. On a farm, rainwater can erode fields. Farmers plow across fields to stop this erosion. The ruts made by the plow keep the water from flowing downhill.

When flowing water slows, sediment is deposited. This happens when rivers reach oceans, lakes, or the bottom of a hill. When a river enters a lake formed by a dam, it can cause a problem. The sediment it drops must be dug out. When a river meets the ocean, the sediment that it drops can form a delta.

The frozen water in a glacier can cause erosion too. Gravity pulls glaciers downhill. As they move, they grind rocks beneath them into sediments. Sediments get carried along by the moving ice.

This river deposits sediment when it reaches the ocean, forming a delta.

How are minerals identified?

Properties of Minerals

To a scientist who studies the Earth, minerals are naturally made solids that can be found in soil and rocks. There are many different minerals, but just a few of them make up most of Earth's rocks.

Minerals can be identified by their properties. Some minerals have a certain smell. Other minerals make tiny bubbles when they touch chemicals called acids.

Hardness

Mohs' scale is used to tell how hard a mineral is. The scale rates the hardness of minerals from 1 to 10. Diamonds are the hardest minerals. They have a hardness of 10.

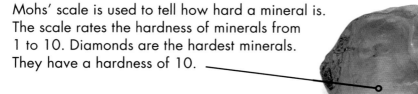

Magnetism

Magnetite, pictured here with iron filings, is strongly magnetic.

Luster

Luster describes the way a mineral's surface reflects light. A glassy luster is shiny like glass. An earthy luster is chalky and dull. This hematite has a metallic luster.

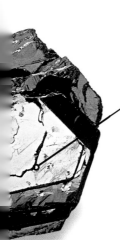

Shape

Some minerals have a definite shape. This pyrite is shaped like cubes.

Streak

Streak is the color of a mineral in its powdered form. To see a mineral's streak, you rub it on a hard, rough, white surface. This is the streak of hematite.

Texture

The texture of a mineral describes the way it feels. This opal has a smooth texture.

Using Properties to Identify Minerals

To identify a mineral, scientists observe and compare, using charts of known minerals. They try to match the mineral they are studying with a known mineral.

The chart below shows the names and properties of some common minerals. Use it to identify minerals shown on the next page.

Mineral	color	texture	smell	luster	hardness	shape	streak
Muscovite	colorless, light-colored	smooth	no	pearly	$2\frac{1}{2}$		white
Fluorite	colorless, pink, purple, green	smooth	no	glassy	4		white
Halite	colorless	smooth	no	glassy	$2\frac{1}{2}$		white
Calcite	white, colorless, pale colors	smooth	no	glassy	3		white
Quartz	clear-white	smooth	no	glassy	7		white
Pyrite	gold	smooth	no	metallic	6–7 (for crystals)		greenish-black
Sulfur	pale to bright yellow	gritty	rotten egg	dull to glassy	$1\frac{1}{2}$ to $2\frac{1}{2}$		white to pale yellow
Talc	white, apple-green, gray	greasy	no	pearly	1		white
Arsenopyrite	brassy white or gray	gritty	garlic	metallic	$5\frac{1}{2}$ to 6		black

- Smooth texture
- Pearly luster
- Hardness of 2.5
- Forms sheets

- Greasy texture
- Pearly luster
- Hardness of 1
- White streak

- Smooth texture
- Hardness of 2.5
- White streak
- Glassy luster

- Gritty texture
- Metallic luster
- Smells like garlic
- Hardness of 5.5 to 6
- Black streak

- Gritty texture
- Dull to glassy luster
- Smells like a rotten egg
- White streak

- Smooth texture
- Glassy luster
- Hardness of 7
- White streak

How are rocks classified?

Igneous Rocks

There are three main types of rocks. Each is formed in a different way. **Igneous** rocks form when melted rock cools and hardens. If rock cools slowly, large crystals of minerals form. If rock cools quickly, small crystals form. Granite is a rock that cools slowly underground. It has large crystals.

Basalt forms when lava is quickly cooled by ocean water. It is a dark green or black rock with small crystals. Pumice forms when lava is quickly cooled by air. Small holes form where gas was trapped in lava as it cooled.

Basalt

Granite

Pumice

Sedimentary Rocks

Most **sedimentary** rocks form when bits of rock and other materials settle on top of each other and harden. The particles become stuck together by natural chemicals.

Sandstone and conglomerate are sedimentary rocks. Sandstone is made up of layers of sand. Conglomerate is made up of larger bits of material pressed together.

Layers of sedimentary rock often hold fossils. Scientists can learn about a plant or animal and its environment by studying the rock around it.

Metamorphic Rocks

Sometimes rocks are changed after they form. Heat and pressure can change how the particles are arranged. New minerals may also form. The rocks that are left by these changes are called **metamorphic** rocks. At high pressure and high temperature, rock particles may form rough layers, as seen in gneiss. At low pressure, thin layers form, as seen in slate.

Conglomerate

Slate

Gneiss

The Rock Cycle

Rocks are always being formed, broken down, or changed. They can change from one type to another in any order. An igneous rock today may become a metamorphic rock in the future. Sometimes they stay in the same form for millions of years. The changes that rocks go through are called the rock cycle. The different ways that one type of rock can become another type of rock are shown below.

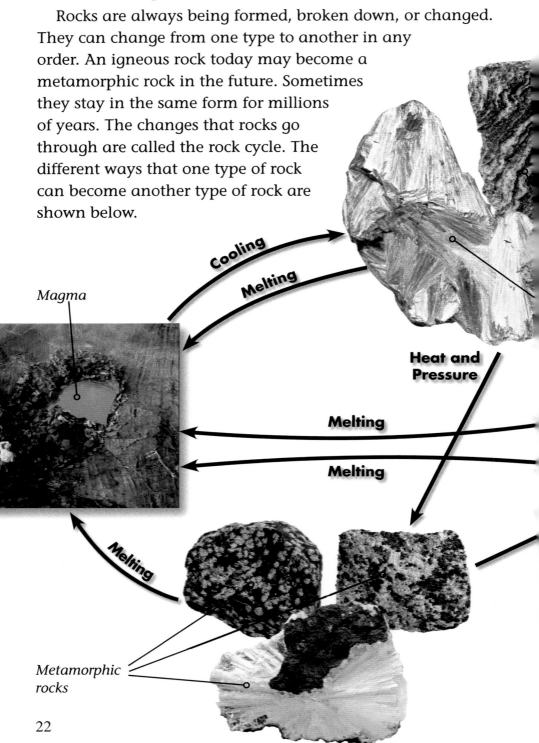

Magma

Cooling

Melting

Heat and Pressure

Melting

Melting

Melting

Metamorphic rocks

Relative Ages of Rocks

Layers of rock are laid down on top of one another over time. The layers close to Earth's surface are younger than the layers below them. Sometimes the layers get turned over or bent by earthquakes, volcanoes, or the formation of mountains. Layers of rock are usually flat. If layers of rock are broken or tilted, it shows that something has happened to move the layers. Layers of rock can show how old one fossil is compared to another. Fossils found in lower layers are older than those in upper layers.

Weathering

Soil

Igneous rocks

Weathering

Weathering

Cementation

Sedimentary rocks

Glossary

chemical weathering   the changing of materials in a rock by chemical processes

core   the center part of Earth that includes the liquid outer core and the solid inner core

crust   Earth's outermost and thinnest layer

igneous   a type of rock formed when melted rocks cool and harden

mantle   the layer of Earth between the crust and the core

mechanical weathering   the breaking down of rock into smaller pieces by any physical force or processes such as gravity, water, wind, ice, or life forms

metamorphic   a type of rock formed when existing rock is changed by heat or pressure

plate   a large section of Earth's crust and upper mantle

sedimentary   a type of rock formed when sediments are pressed and cemented together